# 2012 Conference of the North American Chapter of the Association for Computational Linguistics: Human Language Technologies (NAACL HLT 2012)



## Tutorial Abstracts

Montreal, Quebec, Canada
3 June 2012

ISBN: 978-1-62276-231-6

**Printed from e-media with permission by:**

Curran Associates, Inc.
57 Morehouse Lane
Red Hook, NY 12571

proceedings.com

**Some format issues inherent in the e-media version may also appear in this print version.**



Printed by Curran Associates, Inc. (2012)

For permission requests, please contact the Association for Computational Linguistics at the address below.

Association for Computational Linguistics
209 N. Eighth Street
Stroudsburg, Pennsylvania 18360

Phone: 1-570-476-8006
Fax: 1-570-476-0860

acl@aclweb.org

**Additional copies of this publication are available from:**

Curran Associates, Inc.
57 Morehouse Lane
Red Hook, NY 12571 USA
Phone: 845-758-0400
Fax: 845-758-2634
Email: curran@proceedings.com
Web: www.proceedings.com

# TABLE OF CONTENTS

# T2: Structured Sparsity in Natural Language Processing: Models, Algorithms and Applications

André F. T. Martins, Mário A. T. Figueiredo, and Noah A. Smith

## Abstract

This tutorial will cover recent advances in sparse modeling with diverse applications in natural language processing (NLP). A sparse model is one that uses a relatively small number of features to map an input to an output, such as a label sequence or parse tree. The advantages of sparsity are, among others, compactness and interpretability; in fact, sparsity is currently a major theme in statistics, machine learning, and signal processing. The goal of sparsity can be seen in terms of earlier goals of feature selection and therefore model selection (Della Pietra et al., 1997; Guyon and Elisseeff, 2003; McCallum, 2003).

This tutorial will focus on methods which embed sparse model selection into the parameter estimation problem. In such methods, learning is carried out by minimizing a regularized empirical risk functional composed of two terms: a "loss term," which controls the goodness of fit to the data (e.g., log loss or hinge loss), and a "regularizer term," which is designed to promote sparsity. The simplest example is L1-norm regularization (Tibshirani, 2006), which penalizes weight components individually, and has been explored in various NLP applications (Kazama and Tsujii, 2003; Goodman, 2004; Gao, 2007). More sophisticated regularizers, those that use mixed norms and groups of weights, are able to promote "structured" sparsity: i.e., they promote sparsity patterns that are compatible with a priori knowledge about the structure of the feature space. These kind of regularizers have been proposed in the statistical and signal processing literature (Yuan and Lin, 2006; Zhao et al., 2009; Kim et al., 2010; Bach et al., 2011) and are a recent topic of research in NLP (Eisenstein et al., 2011; Martins et al, 2011, Das and Smith, 2012). Sparsity-inducing regularizers require the use of specialized optimization routines for learning (Wright et al., 2009; Xiao, 2009; Langford et al., 2009).

The tutorial will consist of three parts: (1) how to formulate the problem, i.e., how to choose the right regularizer for the kind of sparsity pattern intended; (2) how to solve the optimization problem efficiently; and (3) examples of the use of sparsity within natural language processing problems.

# OUTLINE

## 1. Introduction

(30 minutes)

- What is sparsity?
- Why sparsity is often desirable in NLP
- Feature selection: wrappers, filters, and embedded methods
- What has been done in other areas: the Lasso and group-Lasso, compressive sensing, and recovery guarantees
- Theoretical and practical limitations of previous methods to typical NLP problems
- Beyond cardinality: structured sparsity

## 2. Group-Lasso and Mixed-Norm Regularizers

(45 minutes)

- Selecting columns in a grid-shaped feature space
- Examples: multiple classes, multi-task learning, multiple kernel learning
- Mixed L2/L1 and $L_{inf}$/L1 norms: the group Lasso
- Non-overlapping groups
- Example: feature template selection
- Tree-structured groups
- The general case: a DAG
- Coarse-to-fine regularization

## 3. Coffee Break

(15 minutes)

## 4. Optimization Algorithms

(45 minutes)

- Non-smooth optimization: limitations of subgradient algorithms
- Quasi-Newton methods: OWL-QN
- Proximal gradient algorithms: iterative soft-thresholding, forward-backward and other splittings
- Computing proximal steps
- Other algorithms: FISTA, Sparsa, ADMM, Bregman iterations
- Convergence rates

- Online algorithms: limitations of stochastic subgradient descent
- Online proximal gradient algorithms
- Managing general overlapping groups
- Memory footprint, time/space complexity, etc.
- The "Sparseptron" algorithm and debiasing

5. **Applications**

   (30 minutes):

   - Sociolinguistic association discovery
   - Sequence problems: named entity recognition, chunking
   - Multilingual dependency parsing
   - Lexicon expansion

6. **Closing Remarks and Discussion**

   (15 minutes)

# BIOS

**André F. T. Martins**
Instituto de Telecomunicações, Instituto Superior Técnico
Av. Rovisco Pais, 1, 1049-001 Lisboa, Portugal,
and Priberam Informática
Al. Afonso Henriques, 41 - 2., 1000-123 Lisboa, Portugal
afm--AT--cs.cmu.edu

A. Martins is a final year Ph.D. student in Carnegie Mellon's School of Computer Science and the Instituto de Telecomunicações at Instituto Superior Técnico, where he is working on a degree in Language Technologies. Martins' research interests include natural language processing, machine learning, convex optimization, and sparse modeling. His dissertation focuses on new models and algorithms for structured prediction with non-local features. His paper "Concise Integer Linear Programming Formulations for Dependency Parsing" received a best paper award at ACL 2009.

**Mário A. T. Figueiredo**
Instituto de Telecomunicações, Instituto Superior Técnico
Av. Rovisco Pais, 1, 1049-001 Lisboa, Portugal
mario.figueiredo--AT--lx.it.pt

M. Figueiredo is a professor of electrical and computer engineering at Instituto Superior Técnico (the engineering school of the Technical University of Lisbon) and his main research interests include machine learning, statistical signal processing, and optimization. He recently guest co-edited a special issue of the IEEE Journal on Special Topics in Signal Processing devoted to compressive sensing (one of the central areas of research on sparsity) and gave several invited talks (and a tutorial at ICASSP 2012) on optimization algorithms for problems involving sparsity.

**Noah A. Smith**
School of Computer Science, Carnegie Mellon University
5000 Forbes Avenue, Pittsburgh, PA 15213, USA
nasmith--AT--cs.cmu.edu

N. Smith is Finmeccanica associate professor in language technologies and machine learning at CMU. His research interests include statistical natural language processing, especially unsupervised methods, machine learning for structured data, and applications of natural language processing, including machine translation and statistical modeling of text and quantitative social data. He recently published a book, Linguistic Structure Prediction, about many of these topics; in 2009 he gave a tutorial at ICML about structured prediction in NLP.

## ACKNOWLEDGMENTS

This tutorial was enabled by support from the following organizations:

- National Science Foundation (USA), CAREER grant IIS-1054319.
- Fundação para a Ciência e Tecnologia (Portugal), grant PEst-OE/EEI/LA0008/2011.
- Fundação para a Ciência e Tecnologia and Information and Communication Technologies Institute (Portugal/USA), through the CMU-Portugal Program.
- QREN/POR Lisboa (Portugal), EU/FEDER programme, Discooperio project, contract 2011/18501.

# T3: Arabic Dialect Processing Tutorial

Mona Diab, Nizar Habash

## ABSTRACT

The existence of dialects for any language constitutes a challenge for NLP in general since it adds another set of variation dimensions from a known standard. The problem is particularly interesting and challenging in Arabic and its different dialects, where the diversion from the standard could, in some linguistic views, warrant a classification as different languages. This problem would not be as pronounced if Modern Standard Arabic (MSA) were the native language of some sub group of Arabic speakers, however it is not. Any realistic and practical approach to processing Arabic will have to account for dialectal usage since it is so pervasive. In this tutorial, we will attempt to highlight different dialectal phenomena, how they migrate from the standard and why they pose challenges to NLP. This area of research (dialects in general and Arabic dialects in particular) is gaining a lot of interest. For example, the DARPA-funded BOLT program starting this year will only consider dialectal varieties for its effort on Arabic. Furthermore, there was a workshop on dialect processing as part of EMNLP 2011.

This tutorial has four different parts: First, we contextualize the question of Arabic dialects from a sociolinguistic and political perspective. Second, we present a discussion of issues in relevant to Arabic NLP; this includes generic issues common to MSA and dialects, and MSA specific issues. In the third part, we detail dialectal linguistic issues and contrast them to MSA issues. In the last part, we review the state-of-the-art in Arabic dialect processing covering several enabling technologies and applications, e.g., dialect identification, speech recognition, morphological processing (analysis, disambiguation, tokenization, POS tagging), parsing, and machine translation. Throughout the presentation we will make references to the different resources available and draw contrastive links with standard Arabic and English. Moreover, we will discuss annotation standards as exemplified in the Treebank. We will provide links to recent publications and available toolkits/resources for all four sections.

This tutorial is designed for computer scientists and linguists alike. No knowledge of Arabic is required (though, we recommend taking a look at Nizar Habash's Arabic NLP tutorialhttp://www1.ccls.columbia.edu/~cadim/presentations.html which will be reviewed as part of the tutorial.)

## OUTLINE

1. **Introduction**

   Introduction to the question of Arabic dialects from sociolinguistic and political perspectives (20 min)

2. **General (Standard/Dialectal) Arabic linguistic issues and their relevance to NLP**

   Orthography, Phonology, Morphology, Syntax (60 min)

3. **Coffee Break**

   (20 min)

4. **Generic dialect issues from an NLP perspective**

   Orthography, Phonology, Morphology, Syntax (40 min)

5. **State-of-the-art in a sample of applications for Arabic dialects**

   Speech recognition, Morphological processing, Parsing, Machine Translation (40 min)

## BIOS

**Mona Diab**
850 Interchurch Center MC 7717
475 Riverside Drive
New York, NY 10115
Office 212-870-1290, Fax 212-870-1285
mdiab--AT--ccls.columbia.edu
http://www1.ccls.columbia.edu/~mdiab/

Mona Diab received her PhD in 2003 in the Linguistics department and UMIACS, University of Maryland College Park. Her PhD work focused on lexical semantic issues and was titled Word Sense Disambiguation within a Multilingual Framework. Mona is currently a research scientist at the Center for Computational Learning Systems, Columbia University. Her research includes work on word sense disambiguation, automatic acquisition of natural language resources such as dictionaries and taxonomies, unsupervised learning methods, lexical semantics, cross language knowledge induction from both parallel and comparable corpora, Arabic NLP in general, tools for processing Arabic(s), computational modeling of Arabic dialects, Arabic syntactic and semantic parsing.

**Nizar Habash**
850 Interchurch Center MC 7717
475 Riverside Drive
New York, NY 10115
Office 212-870-1289, Fax 212-870-1285
habash@ccls.columbia.edu
http://www.nizarhabash.com

Nizar Habash received his PhD in 2003 from the Computer Science Department, University of Maryland College Park. His Ph.D. thesis is titled Generation-Heavy Hybrid Machine Translation. He is currently a research scientist at the Center for Computational Learning Systems in Columbia University. His research includes work on machine translation, natural language generation, lexical semantics, morphological analysis, generation and disambiguation, computational modeling of Arabic dialects, and Arabic dialect parsing. Nizar recently published a book entitled "Introduction to Arabic Natural Language Processing".

# T4: Natural Language Processing in Watson

## ABSTRACT

Open domain Question Answering (QA) is a long standing research problem. Recently, IBM took on this challenge in the context of the Jeopardy! game. Jeopardy! is a well-known TV quiz show that has been airing on television in the United States for more than 25 years. It pits three human contestants against one another in a competition that requires answering rich natural language questions over a very broad domain of topics. The development of a system able to compete to grand champions in the Jeopardy! challenge led to the design of the DeepQA architecture and the implementation of Watson. The DeepQA project shapes a grand challenge in Computer Science that aims to illustrate how the wide and growing accessibility of natural language content and the integration and advancement of Natural Language Processing, Information Retrieval, Machine Learning, Knowledge Representation and Reasoning, and massively parallel computation can drive open-domain automatic Question Answering technology to a point where it clearly and consistently rivals the best human performance. Natural Language Processing (NLP) plays a crucial role in the overall Deep QA architecture. It allows to "make sense" of both question and unstructured knowledge contained in the large corpora where most of the answers are located. That's why we decided to focus this tutorial on the NLP technology adopted by Watson and on how it fits in the general Deep QA architecture.

## OUTLINE

The course is structured in two modules (1.5h each), described below.

1. **Module 1 An overview of the Deep QA project**

   This lesson provides a general introduction to the Deep QA project, addressing the following topics

   1. Analysis of the Jeopardy Task
   2. The Deep QA architecture
   3. Development Cycle
2. **Module 2 Natural Language Processing in Watson**

   This lesson focuses on the NLP technology implemented in Watson, highlighting the advancements with respect to state of the art techniques in Question Answering. In particular:

1. Role of NLP in the Deep QA architecture
2. UIMA
3. Passage Scoring
4. Prismatic

# BIOS

Instructors will be Research Staff Members from the Algorithms team developing Watson at IBM Research. Depending on availability for the specific day of the tutorial, they will be one or more from the following list:

**Alfio M. Gliozzo**
19 Skyline Drive, Hawthorne, NY 10532
phone: +1-917-744-4351
gliozzo--AT--us.ibm.com
https://researcher.ibm.com/researcher/view.php?person=us-gliozzo

Dr. Alfio Gliozzo is Research Staff Member at IBM Research, where he is part of the Deep QA team. His main research focus is Domain Adaptation of Question Answering systems using machine learning and knowledge acquisition. He is author of about 50 publications in the areas of Computational Linguistics, Information Retrieval, and Semantic Web.

**Aditya Kalyanpur**
19 Skyline Drive, Hawthorne, NY 10532
adityakal--AT--us.ibm.com
http://researcher.ibm.com/researcher/view.php?person=us-adityakal

Aditya Kalyanpur is a Research Staff Member at IBM Research. His research interests include knowledge representation & reasoning, ontologies, natural language processing, machine learning and statistical data mining. Aditya has been involved in the development of several core algorithms in Watson related to question analysis, evidence gathering and scoring, knowledge based inference, and answer merging and ranking.

**James Fan**
19 Skyline Drive, Hawthorne, NY 10532
fanj--AT--us.ibm.com
https://researcher.ibm.com/researcher/view.php?person=us-fanj

James Fan is a research staff member at IBM Research. James has been working in the area of question answering since 2003, and has published on subjects in knowledge representation, reasoning, natural language processing and machine learning. James is currently working the DeepQA project.

# T5: Variational Inference for Structured NLP Models

David Burkett, Dan Klein

## Abstract

Historically, key breakthroughs in structured NLP models, such as chain CRFs or PCFGs, have relied on imposing careful constraints on the locality of features in order to permit efficient dynamic programming for computing expectations or finding the highest-scoring structures. However, as modern structured models become more complex and seek to incorporate longer-range features, it is more and more often the case that performing exact inference is impossible (or at least impractical) and it is necessary to resort to some sort of approximation technique, such as beam search, pruning, or sampling. In the NLP community, one increasingly popular approach is the use of variational methods for computing approximate distributions.

The goal of the tutorial is to provide an introduction to variational methods for approximate inference, particularly mean field approximation and belief propagation. The intuition behind the mathematical derivation of variational methods is fairly simple: instead of trying to directly compute the distribution of interest, first consider some efficiently computable approximation of the original inference problem, then find the solution of the approximate inference problem that minimizes the distance to the true distribution. Though the full derivations can be somewhat tedious, the resulting procedures are quite straightforward, and typically consist of an iterative process of individually updating specific components of the model, conditioned on the rest. Although we will provide some theoretical background, the main goal of the tutorial is to provide a concrete procedural guide to using these approximate inference techniques, illustrated with detailed walkthroughs of examples from recent NLP literature.

Once both variational inference procedures have been described in detail, we'll provide a summary comparison of the two, along with some intuition about which approach is appropriate when. We'll also provide a guide to further exploration of the topic, briefly discussing other variational techniques, such as expectation propagation and convex relaxations, but concentrating mainly on providing pointers to additional resources for those who wish to learn more.

## Outline

1. **Introduction**
    1. Approximate inference background
    2. Definition of variational inference
    3. Structured NLP problem setting, loglinear models
    4. Graphical model notation, feature locality
2. **Mean Field Approximation**
    1. General description and theoretical background
    2. Derivation of updates for simple two-variable model
    3. Structured mean field: extension to joint CRFs
    4. Joint parsing and word alignment
    5. High level description of other models (Coref, Nonparametric Bayes)
3. **Belief Propagation**
    1. General description and theoretical background
    2. Factor graph notation
    3. Formulas for messages and beliefs, with joint CRF example
    4. Dependency parsing
    5. Word alignment
4. **Wrap-up**
    1. Mean Field vs Belief Propagation (i.e. what to use when)
    2. Other variational methods
    3. Additional resources

## BIOS

**David Burkett**
University of California, Berkeley
dburkett--AT--cs.berkeley.edu

David Burkett is a Ph.D. candidate in the Computer Science Division at the University of California, Berkeley. The main focus of his research is on modeling syntactic agreement in bilingual corpora. His interests are diverse, though, and he has worked on parsing, phrase alignment, language evolution, coreference resolution, and even video game AI. He has worked as an instructional assistant for multiple AI courses at Berkeley and won the Outstanding Graduate Student Instructor award in 2009.

**Dan Klein**
University of California, Berkeley
klein--AT--cs.berkeley.edu

Dan Klein is an Associate Professor of Computer Science at the University of California, Berkeley. His research includes many areas of statistical natural language processing, including grammar induction, parsing, machine translation, information extraction, document summarization, historical linguistics, and speech recognition. His academic awards include a Sloan Fellowship, a Microsoft Faculty Fellowship, an NSF CAREER Award, the ACM Grace Murray Hopper Award, Best Paper Awards at ACL, EMNLP and NAACL, and the UC Berkeley Distinguished Teaching Award.

# T6: Processing modality and negation

Roser Morante, CLiPS - University of Antwerp, Belgium

## ABSTRACT


### 1.1 Tutorial content

Modality and negation are ubiquitous phenomena in language. Generally speaking, modality is a grammatical category that allows to express aspects related to the speaker's attitude towards her statements in terms of degree of certainty, reliability, and subjectivity. In this tutorial modality is understood in a broad sense, which involves related concepts like subjectivity, hedging, evidentiality, uncertainty, committed belief, and factuality. Negation is a grammatical category that allows to change the truth value of a proposition. Modality and negation are treated together because they are interrelated phenomena and are protypically expressed by linguistic devices that share some formal characteristics. For example, modality and negation cues function as operators that scope over certain parts of the sentence.

From a natural language processing perspective, a very relevant aspect of modality and negation is that they encode extra-propositional aspects of meaning. While traditionally most research has focused on propositional aspects of meaning, the interest in processing extra-propositonal aspects has grown in recent years, as a natural consequence of the consolidation of areas that focus on the computational treatment of propositional aspects. Given a sentence, researchers aim at going beyond determining 'who/what does what to whom/what where and when', which would be the goal of a typical semantic role labeling or event extraction task, and are interested in finding also features such as the source, certainty level, epistemological type, truth value, and subjective aspects of the statements contained in a text. Additionally, researchers are also interested in analysing discourse level phenomena such as finding contradictions and textual entailments or modelling how the status of events changes throughout a text. Modality and negation play a main role in these phenomena.

That there is growing interest in these topics among the NLP community is reflected by a number of recent publications, the edition of the workshop 'Negation and Speculation in Natural Language Processing (NeSp-NLP 2010)', as well as the popularity of the CoNLL 2010 shared task on 'Learning to detect hedges and their scope in natural language tex't and the future publication of a special issue of the journal Computational Linguistics. Research on modality and negation has also been stimulated by the release of a number of data sets annotated with various types of information related to these phenomena.

This tutorial is divided in five modules. In Module 1, I will introduce modality and negation as devices that express extra-propositional aspects of meaning, I will define related concepts and I will show why it is interesting and complex to process them. In Module 2, I will present different categorisation schemes and annotation efforts, as well as an overview of existing resources. In Module 3, I will describe how several related tasks have been modelled and solved. I will present in detail the rule-based and machine learning approaches that have been used to solve the tasks. In Module 4, I will focus on applications that have incorporated the treatment of modality and negation, and on research that analyses the impact of processing these phenomena. The applications range from sentiment analysis to biomedical text mining. Finally, in Module 5, I will summarize achievements and point out open problems.

## 1.2 Relevance for the ACL community

Processing modality and negation is relevant for the ACL community because of several reasons. First, the treatment of modality and negation is very relevant for all NLP applications that involve text understanding. This includes applications that need to discriminate between factual and non-factual information (uncertain facts, opinions, attitudes, emotions, and beliefs), like information extraction, opinion mining, sentiment analysis, (biomedical) text mining, or question answering, as well as other applications that process the meaning of texts, like recognizing textual entailment, paraphrasing, or summarization. Incorporating information about modality and negation has been shown to be useful for a number of applications, such as biomedical text processing (Friedman et al., 1994; Di Marco and Mercer, 2005; Mutalik et al., 2001; Chapman et al., 2001), opinion mining and sentiment analysis (Wilson et al., 2005a), recognizing textual entailment (Marneffe et al., 2006; Snow et al., 2006), and automatic style checking (Ganter and Strube, 2009). Hence this topic is of general importance to the NLP community as a whole, as evidenced by the fact that a number of researchers and groups are currently working on this phenomena.

Second, this topic has received a noticeable boost from several recent events: the workshop Negation and Speculation in Natural Language Processing (NeSp-NLP 2010), which I co-organized in Uppsala just before ACL 2010; the CoNLL Shared Task 2010 on Learning to detect hedges and their scope in natural language text, which attracted 51 submissions from 23 teams; and the publication of the Special Issue on Modality and Negation by the journal Computational Linguistics, that will appear at the end of 2011. This SI has received a considerable number of submissions, which shows that the community is active in treating these phenomena. Research on modality and negation is also supported by the fact that a number of data sets annotated with various aspects of modality and negation information have been made available, such as the MPQA Opinion Corpus (Wiebe et al., 2005), Rubinâ€™s (2006; 2007) certainty corpus, the ACE 2008 corpus (Linguistic Data Consortium, 2008), and the FactBank corpus (2009), the BioScope corpus (Vincze et al., 2008).

Given that there is clearly substantial interest in this topic from the ACL community and given that the research on this area is evolving quickly, I believe that the proposed tutorial will help attendees to keep up to date with recent advances in the field and discover new directions for future research.

# OUTLINE

1. **Introduction: modality and negation as extra-propositional aspects of meaning**
    1. Defining modality
    2. Concepts related to modality: hedging, evidentiality, uncertainty, factuality, subjectivity, non-committed belief
    3. Defining negation
    4. Negation versus negative polarity
    5. Why is it interesting to process modality and negation?
    6. Complex aspects of processing modality and negation
2. **Categorising and annotating negation and modality**
    1. Annotation schemes
    2. Existing resources
    3. Future directions
3. **Tasks related to processing modality and negation**
    1. Cue detection
    2. Detecting speculated sentences
    3. Scope resolution
    4. Finding negated/speculated events
    5. Modality tagging
    6. Belief categorisation
    7. Processing contradiction and contrast
    8. Incorporating negation/modality in parsers
4. **Modality and negation in applications**
    1. Sentiment analysis
    2. Recognizing textual entailment
    3. Machine translation
    4. Text mining
5. **Open problems and discussion**

# BIO

**Roser Morante**
Computational Linguistics and Psycholinguistics (CLiPS) Research Center
University of Antwerp
Email: roser.morante --AT-- ua dot ac dot be
http://www.clips.ua.ac.be/~roser/

Dr. Roser Morante is a senior researcher at CLiPS, a research center associated with the Linguistics Department of the Faculty of Arts at the University of Antwerp, Belgium. She obtained her PhD in Computational Linguistics at the University of Tilburg, The Netherlands, where she also worked as a postdoctoral researcher. She is currently working on the Biograph project led by Professor Walter Daelemans, where she applies text mining techniques to extract biomedical relations from scientific texts. In the project she has worked extensively on both modality and negation. She proposed the first model of the scope finding task as a machine learning classification task and has developed systems for finding the scope of negation and hedge cues. The system that her team submitted to the CoNLL Shared Task 2010 scored first in Task 2 on finding the scope of hedge cues. She has co-oganized the Workshop on Negation and Speculation in Natural Language Processing (NeSp-NLP 2010) and she is currently a Guest Editor of the Special Issue on Modality and Negation for the journal Computational Linguistics. She has also been involved in the organization of the Workshop Advances on Bio Text Mining 2010, the SemEval 2010 shared task on Linking Events and Their Participants in Discourse, and the evaluation exercise Processing modality and negation for machine reading, a pilot task of the Question Answering for Machine Reading Evaluation at CLEF 2011.

My research interests revolve around applying supervised machine learning techniques to semantics oriented natural language processing tasks at sentence and document level, like semantic role labeling, relation extraction, coreference resolution, paraphrasing, or textual entailment. In the past I have worked on machine translation, dialogue systems and semantic role labeling. At this moment I am working mostly on biomedical text mining: processing negation and modality, extraction of biomedical events, extraction of protein-protein interactions, semantic role labeling, and coreference resolution.

# T7: On-Demand Distributional Semantic Distance and Paraphrasing

Yuval Marton

## ABSTRACT

Semantic distance measures aim to answer questions such as: How close in meaning are words A and B? Fore example: "couch" and "sofa"? (very); "wave" and "ripple"? (so-so); "wave" and "bank"? (far). Distributional measures do that by modeling which words occur next to A and next to B in large corpora of text, and then comparing these models of A and B (based on the "Distributional Hypothesis"). Paraphrase generation is the task of finding B (or a set of B's) given A. Semantic distance measures can be used for both paraphrase detection and generation, in assessing this closeness between A and B. Both semantic measures and paraphrasing methods are extensible to other textual units such as phrases, sentences, or documents.

Paraphrase detection and generation have been gaining traction in various NLP subfields, including:

- Statistical machine translation (e.g., phrase table expansion)
- MT evaluation (e.g., TERp or Meteor)
- Search, information retrieval and information extraction (e.g., query expansion)
- Question answering and Watson-like applications (e.g., passage or document clustering)
- Event extraction / event discovery / machine reading (e.g, fitting to existing frames)
- Ontology expansion (e.g., WordNet)
- Language modeling (e.g., semantic LM)
- Textual entailment
- (Multi-)document summarization and natural language generation
- Sentiment analysis and opinion / social network mining (e.g., expansion of positive and negative classes)
- Computational cognitive modeling

This tutorial concentrates on paraphrasing words and short word sequences, a.k.a. "phrases" -- and doing so overcoming previous working memory and representation limitations. We focus on distributional paraphrasing (Pasca and Dienes 2005; Marton et al., 2009; Marton, to appear 2012). We will also cover pivot paraphrasing (Bannard and Callison-Burch, 2005).

We will discuss several weaknesses of distributional paraphrasing, and where the state-of-the-art is. The most notable weakness of distributional paraphrasing is its tendency to rank high antonymous (e.g., big-small) and ontological sibling (e.g., cow-sheep) paraphrase candidates. What qualitative improvement can we hope to achieve with growing size of monolingual texts? What else can be done to ameliorate this problem? (Mohammad et al., EMNLP 2008; Hovy, 2010; Marton et al., WMT 2011).

Another potential weakness is the difficulty in detecting and generating longer-than-word (phrasal) paraphrases, because pre-calculating a collocation matrix for phrases becomes prohibitive in the matrix size with longer phrases, even with sparse representation. Unless all phrases are known in advance, this becomes a problem for real-world applications.

We will present an alternative to pre-calculation: on-demand paraphrasing, as described in Marton (to appear 2012). There, searching the monolingual text resource is done on-demand with a suffix array or prefix tree with suffix links (Manber and Myers, 1993; Gusfield, 1997; Lopez, 2007). This enables constructing large vector representation, since there is no longer a need to compute a whole matrix. Searching for paraphrase candidates can be done in a reasonable amount of time and memory, for phrases and paraphrases of an arbitrary maximal length. The resulting technique enables using richer -- and hence, potentially more accurate -- representations (including higher-dimension tensors). It opens up a great potential for further gains in research and product systems alike, from SMT to search and IR, event discovery, and many other NLP areas.

# T8: Predicting Structures in NLP: Constrained Conditional Models and Integer Linear Programming NLP

Dan Goldwasser, Vivek Srikumar, Dan Roth

## ABSTRACT

Making decisions in natural language processing problems often involves assigning values to sets of interdependent variables where the expressive dependency structure can influence, or even dictate what assignments are possible. This setting includes a broad range of structured prediction problems such as semantic role labeling, named entity and relation recognition, co-reference resolution, dependency parsing and semantic parsing. The setting is also appropriate for cases that may require making global decisions that involve multiple components, possibly pre-designed or pre-learned, as in summarization, paraphrasing, textual entailment and question answering. In all these cases, it is natural to formulate the decision problem as a constrained optimization problem, with an objective function that is composed of learned models, subject to domain or problem specific constraints.

Constrained Conditional Models (CCM) formulation of NLP problems (also known as: Integer Linear Programming for NLP) is a learning and inference framework that augments the learning of conditional (probabilistic or discriminative) models with declarative constraints (written, for example, using a first-order representation). The key advantage of the CCM formulation is its support for making decisions in an expressive output space while maintaining modularity and tractability of training and inference. In most applications of this framework in NLP, following [Roth & Yih, CoNLL'04], integer linear programming (ILP) has been used as the inference framework, although other algorithms can be used.

This framework has attracted much attention within the NLP community over the last few years, with multiple papers in all the recent major conferences. Formulating structured prediction as a constrained optimization problem over the output of learned models has several advantages. It allows the incorporation of problem specific global constraints using a first order language â€“ thus freeing the developer from (much of the) low level feature engineering â€“ and guarantees exact inference. Importantly, it provides also the freedom of decoupling model generation (learning) from the constrained inference stage, often simplifying the learning stage as well as the engineering aspect of building an NLP system, while improving the quality of the solutions. These advantages and the availability of off-the-shelf solvers have led to a large variety of NLP tasks being formulated within it, including semantic role labeling, syntactic parsing, co-reference resolution, summarization, transliteration and joint information extraction.

The goal of this tutorial is to introduce the framework of Constrained Conditional Models to the broader ACL community, motivate it as a generic framework for structured inference in global NLP decision problems, present some of the key theoretical and practical issues involved in using CCMs and survey some of the existing applications of it as a way to promote further development of the framework and additional applications. The tutorial will be useful for senior and junior researchers who are interested in structured prediction and global decision problems in NLP, providing a concise overview of recent perspectives and research results.

# OUTLINE

After briefly motivating and introducing the general framework, the main part of the tutorial is a methodological presentation of some of the key computational issues studied within CCMs that we will present by looking at case studies published in the NLP literature. In the last part of the tutorial, we will discuss engineering issues that arise in using CCMs.

1. **Motivation**

   We will begin by introducing structured prediction with various NLP examples. We will motivate the framework of Constrained Conditional Models using examples from sequential inference, sentence compression and semantic role labeling. [30 min]

2. **Examples of Existing CCM Applications**

   We will present several applications that use CCMs â€“ including co-reference resolution, sentence compression and information extraction and use these to explain several of the key advantages the framework offers. In this context, we will discuss several ways in which expressive constraints can be introduced into an application. [30 min]

3. **Modeling CCMs: Inference methods and Constraints**

   We will present and discuss several possibilities for modeling inference in CCMs. We will discuss ways to model problems as structured prediction problems and the use of hard and soft constraints to represent prior knowledge. We will look at ways in which Constrained Conditional Models can be used to augment probabilistic models with declarative knowledge based constraints and how these support expressive global decisions. We will also mention various possibilities for performing the inference, from commercial Integer Linear Programming packages to search techniques to Lagrangian relaxation approximation methods. [30 min]

4. **Training Paradigms**

   The objective function used by CCMs can be decomposed and learned in several ways, ranging from â€œstandardâ€ structured learning, i.e., a complete joint training of the model along with the constraints, to a complete decoupling between the learning and the inference stage. We will present the advantages and disadvantages offered by different training paradigms and provide theoretical and experimental understanding. In this part, we will also compare CCMs to other approaches studied in the literature. [30 min]

5. **Beyond Supervised Learning**

   In the standard supervised setting, we require a corpus that is annotated with the structures of interest, which is expensive and often impractical. In this part of the tutorial, we will show how to go beyond the supervised setting using CCMs, which provide ways to use declarative constraints to guide supervised and semi-supervised training in the presence of partial and indirect supervision. We will also present recent advances in training structured predictors indirectly using a data for a companion binary task. We will review several successful applications of these methods in diverse tasks such as information extraction and textual entailment. [30 min]

6. **Developing CCMs Applications**

   We will present a â€œcookbook approachâ€ for developing applications within the CCM framework and discuss templates for possible applications. [30 min]

# Bios

**Dan Goldwasser**
Computer Science Department, University of Illinois at Urbana-Champaign, IL, 61801
Email: goldwas1--AT--illinois.edu
Phone: +(217) 333-2584

Dan Goldwasser is a PhD candidate in the Department of Computer Science at the University of Illinois at Urbana-Champaign. He is the recipient of the 2010 C.L. and Jane Liu Award for research promise. He published several papers in natural language processing, machine learning and semantic interpretation. His research work studies the role that an external context, such as the real world or a simulated world, plays in semantic interpretation and learning protocols.

**Vivek Srikumar**
Computer Science Department, University of Illinois at Urbana-Champaign, IL. 61801
Email: vsrikum2--AT--illinois.edu
Phone: +(217) 333-2584

Vivek Srikumar is a Ph.D. candidate at the University of Illinois, Urbana-Champaign. He has worked on Machine Learning in the context of Natural Language Processing and has published papers in several conferences. His research deals with applying structure learning and prediction formalized as Constrained Conditional Models to semantic role labeling and its extensions.

**Dan Roth**
Computer Science Department, University of Illinois at Urbana-Champaign, IL, 61801
Email: danr--AT--cs.uiuc.edu
Phone: +(217) 244-7068

Dan Roth is a Professor in the Department of Computer Science at the University of Illinois at Urbana-Champaign and the Beckman Institute of Advanced Science and Technology (UIUC) and a University of Illinois Scholar. He is a fellow of AAAI and the ACM. Roth has published broadly in machine learning, natural language processing, knowledge representation and reasoning and received several paper, teaching and research awards. He has developed several machine learning based natural language processing systems that are widely used in the computational linguistics community and in industry and has presented invited talks and tutorials in several major conferences. Dan Roth has written the first paper on formulating global NLP decisions as ILP problems with his student Scott Yih, presented in CoNLL'04, and since then has worked on further developing Constrained Conditional Models, on learning and inference issues within this framework and on applying it to several NLP problems, including Semantic Role Labeling, Information and Relation Extraction and Transliteration.

# AUTHOR INDEX